PHONICS

for 5th Grade

Children's Reading & Writing Education Books

All Rights reserved. No part of this book may be reproduced or used in any way or form or by any means whether electronic or mechanical, this means that you cannot record or photocopy any material ideas or tips that are provided in this book.

Copyright 2016

Read and rewrite the following words.

ee cheese
CHēz

bee

eel

fee

see

beef

been

beep

oa   boat
bōt

oat

oak

oat

boat

coat

coax

foal

ea clean
klēn

dead
deaf
head
lead
ahead
bread
dealt

oe backhoe
ˈbakˌhō

doe

foe

hoe

toe

woe

aloe

goes

oo school
skōol

cool
foot
loose
tool
root
loop
drool

ai brain
    brān

pain

gain

faith

maid

main

laid

fair

ow snow
snō

row

show

bow

slow

grow

blow

own

ue   blue
     bloo

due
clue
true
glue
hue
cue
issue

gr- grass
gras

great

green

grasp

grade

grip

gray

ground

sc- scale
skāl

school
scheme
scared
scum
scream
scout
score

pr- pretzel
pretsəl

glaze

gleam

glow

glare

glue

glade

glitch

sl - slipper
ˈslipər

sky
ski
skin
task
ask
mask
flask

pl- **plug**
pləg

pray
proud
prone
preach
priest
press
prove

sm-

smock
smäk

slide
slow
slime
slam
slid
sleep
slim

br- brown
broun

place

play

plunge

plot

please

plum

plow

dr- drum
drəm

smack

smear

small

smoke

smog

smudge

smell

bl-   block
      bläk

bride

broke

brail

bread

brag

bridge

breeze

tr- train
trān

dry
dream
drive
drill
drop
drag
dread

cr- crab
krab

bliss

blood

blow

blank

bless

blur

blame

fr- fruit
froot

trash

tree

trip

truss

treat

trim

troll

cl- cloud
kloud

crisp

cream

crave

crane

crow

crush

crash

fl - fly
flī

fry
friend
freckle
fresh
frown
frog
freak

ch- chain
CHān

claw

clown

clear

clip

clutch

clone

clap

-ch   switch
swiCH

flaw

flee

flow

flu

flip

flock

flick

sh- shark
SHärk

chess

chose

chain

chuckle

chest

chip

choke

-sh trash
traSH

clutch

hatch

fetch

watch

pooch

much

rich

th - 3　　three
　　　　　　THrē

shell

show

shed

ship

shut

shake

shiedl

-th earth
ərTH

wash

trash

mush

wish

push

leash

fish

wh- wheel
(h)wēl

thin

thick

thaw

throw

thief

thirst

thug

-ck duck
dək

myth

wealth

health

moth

birth

cloth

growth

ph- photo /fōtō/

whip

whose

whack

whisk

when

what

where

-tch 🕐 **watch**
wäCH

rock

flock

tick

wreck

sock

pick

pack

kn-  knife
nīf

phase
phone
phobia
phew
phonics
pharaoh
phenomena

-ng   ring / riNG

clucth

dutch

match

witch

fetch

glitch

hatch

qu- **queen**
kwēn

know

knit

knock

kneel

knick

knack

knot

-ll ball
bôl

thing

wing

thong

rang

hung

bring

wrong

www.ingramcontent.com/pod-product-compliance
Lightning Source LLC
LaVergne TN
LVHW082254070426
835507LV00037B/2285